Whitney Levin

AF691972

COMPUTER YELLOW PAGES

FOR STUDENTS AND TEACHERS

by Frances C. Blackburn

Incentive Publications, Inc.
Nashville, Tennessee

If learning is an act of exploration, then technology
equips the explorer for the journey of a lifetime . . .
Technology: opening minds with a new set of keys
(Unknown)

For my brother John Crow,
the Computer Wizard, who built my first computer.
He gave me the keys that started me on
the most exciting journey of my life!

Cover by Marta Drayton
Edited by Jennifer E. Janke

Library of Congress Catalog Card Number: 99-71592
ISBN 0-86530-439-4

Copyright ©1999 by Incentive Publications, Inc., Nashville, TN. All rights reserved. No part of this publication may be reproduced, stored in a retrieval system, or transmitted in any form or by any means (electronic, mechanical, photocopying, recording, or otherwise) without written permission from Incentive Publications, Inc.

Table of Contents

Introduction

About 5 years ago, I experienced a cataclysmic event that changed my life; I got my first computer. I say "cataclysmic" because it truly caused me to change my whole way of thinking about a lot of things. All of a sudden, I have a wonderful piece of modern technology that is supposed to lighten my workload by helping me to average my grades, generate progress reports, and spit out worksheets and tests. But as with all great solutions, there must first be a problem. My problem was—How do I turn it on? I had an instruction manual, and for the first time since I was six years old, I was faced with a page of words that made absolutely no sense whatsoever to me. Reading computer and software manuals makes us all realize the distinctive language of technology.

Most of my teaching experience has been with primary children. Therefore, I have a vast experience with emerging readers. So, I knew all the word attack skills. I could break the words down into syllables and sound them out, and I taught new vocabulary words in context. But what do you do when none of the context makes sense? If I was going to get anything from my computer, I needed to broaden my computer language base!

The language of technology is the root cause of computer fear, a disease not uncommon to those who are new to technology. Teachers are especially susceptible to this malady. It is very hard for us to ask for assistance; to admit we do not know! Once we begin learning something new, most of us want to know everything about it. We often feel that if we do not know everything, then we know nothing.

Teachers promote lifelong learning as an ideal for students to strive toward. Technology puts this ideal into perspective, because technology is constantly evolving and we must accept the fact that no one person will know everything there is to know about a computer. What is "state of the art" today is obsolete tomorrow, so it forces us to work harder to keep pace with the changes as they occur and embrace the true spirit of lifelong learning.

"Technology: opening minds with a new set of keys."

I don't have a complete set of keys yet, and probably never will. But I am trying to acquire as many as I can. I am growing to realize that I am no longer the "sage on the stage", but rather a "guide on the side." My journey is still very exciting. I hope I never lose that feeling of amazement and awe that I feel when I discover some new "thing" I can do with my computer. It is the same excitement that we see in a child's eyes when "the lightbulb goes on." All of a sudden I find some little something that makes sense. Slowly and surely my keys are beginning to work!

While computers are amazing machines, they can never take the place of books in teaching beginning reading, writing, and computation skills. Computers are enhancements to learning for children. They must never be conceived as toys, but children must respect them as they do the other learning materials in the classroom. It is my sincere desire to help you in your quest to learn computer applications as they may apply to your students and your classroom. I hope you find this guide helpful.

WHAT DOES A TEACHER NEED TO KNOW TO BE "TECHNOLOGY-LITERATE"?

The International Society for Technology in Education (ISTE) has identified standards for technology proficiency for candidates entering the teaching profession. These standards are based on an understanding of the basic concepts involved in the operation of a computer system, using technology applications to enhance personal and professional growth, and applying technology to support the instructional strategies used for their subject and/or grade level. These same skills must be applied to those who are inservice teachers. Teachers who have not received training in the use of the computer must realize their responsibility to stay current with the trends of society! As Arthur Clarke stated, "We must prepare children for their future, not our past." School systems must accept the responsibility and the challenge to provide adequate staff development opportunities for these teachers to feel comfortable with technology.

ISTE'S RECOMMENDED FOUNDATIONS IN TECHNOLOGY FOR ALL TEACHERS

Basic Computer/Technology Operations and Concepts.

Identified skills would include being able to:

1. Operate a multimedia computer system with related peripheral devices to successfully install and use a variety of software packages.

2. Use terminology related to computers and technology appropriately in written and oral communications.

3. Describe and implement basic troubleshooting techniques for multimedia computer systems with related peripheral devices.

4. Use imaging devices such as scanners, digital cameras, and/or video cameras with computer systems and software.

5. Demonstrate knowledge of uses of computers and technology in business, industry, & society.

Personal and Professional Use of Technology.

These competencies would involve being able to:

1. Use productivity tools for word processing, database management, and spreadsheet applications.

2. Apply productivity tools for creating multimedia presentations.

3. Use computer-based technologies including telecommunications to access information and enhance personal and professional productivity.

4. Use computers to support problem solving, data collection, information management, communications, presentations, and decision making.

5. Demonstrate awareness of resources for adaptive assistive devices for students with special needs.

6. Demonstrate knowledge of equity, ethics, legal, and human issues concerning use of computers and technology.

7. Identify computer and related technology resources for facilitating lifelong learning and emerging roles of the learner and the educator.

8. Observe demonstrations or uses of broadcast instruction, audio/video conferencing, and other distant learning applications.

Application of Technology in Instruction.

Identified skills are:

1. Explore, evaluate, and use computer/technology resources including applications, tools, educational software and associated documentation.

2. Describe current instructional principles, research, and appropriate assessment practices as related to the use of computers and technology resources in the curriculum.

3. Design, deliver, and assess student learning activities that integrate computers/technology for a variety of student group strategies and for diverse student populations.

4. Design student learning activities that foster equitable, ethical, and legal use of technology by students.

5. Practice responsible, ethical and legal use of technology, information, and software resources.

©1998, International Society for Technology in Education, 800.336.5191, cust_svc@iste.org, www.iste.org. Reprinted with permission.

WHAT DOES A STUDENT NEED TO KNOW TO BE "TECHNOLOGY-LITERATE"?

There is widespread agreement among the public and educators that students need to achieve computer literacy. Unfortunately, the productivity side of computer use in the general content area is neglected and/or underdeveloped in our schools today. However, there is a shift toward integrating computers into the content areas. Computer skills must relate to content area and classroom assignments, and should be presented in a logical and systematic information process model. (For help in this area see "Computer Skills for Information Problem-Solving: Learning and Teaching Technology in Context.", by Michael B.Eisenberg and Doug Johnson, 1996) Computers in the classroom should be more than a method of rewarding students for good behavior or free time from class.

The guidelines to achieving computer literacy are based on the following:

1. **Access.** In many schools there is not an even distribution of computers among all classrooms. It is possible for a child to complete elementary school without ever having had an opportunity to have hands-on experience with a computer.

2. **Equity**. Schools should be active in giving technology experiences to students who have less access to technology in their homes.

3. **Involvement**. It is important to encourage and support teachers as they "buy in" to new teaching strategies and practices. Many teachers have a great deal of computer fear, due to lack of training and experience. Additional staff development is needed for those teachers who are less knowledgeable of computer operations and applications.

NATIONAL STANDARDS FOR TECHNOLOGY-LITERATE STUDENTS

The Clinton Administration created "The President's Educational Technology Initiative," which recognizes that technology is the key to preparing children to meet the needs of the workplace they will enter in the 21st century. The initiative has "set a new challenge for America: we are calling on parents, teachers, leading CEOs and others to join us in a new national mission. We need schools equipped with the right technology."

The initiative identifies four objectives to be achieved in meeting this challenge. They are that:

1. Modern computers and learning devices will be accessible to every student.

2. Classrooms will be connected to one another and to the outside world.

3. Educational software will be an integral part of the curriculum, and as engaging as the best video game.

4. Teachers will be ready to use and teach technology.

The International Society for Technology in Education (ISTE) is currently formulating National Educational Technology Standards for Students. Sponsors of this project are the National Air and Space Administration (NASA), the U.S. Department of Education, and Apple Computer, Inc. The standards include:

PreK-Grade 5

1. Students will be able to perform basic operations and have an understanding of concepts associated with technology.
2. Students will show an awareness of social, ethical, and human issues with knowledge acquired through technology.
3. Students will exhibit proficiency in the use of technology productivity tools.
4. Students will exhibit proficiency in the use of technology communications tools.
5. Students will exhibit proficiency in the use of technology research tools.
6. Students will exhibit proficiency in the use of technology problem-solving and decision-making tools.

The following objectives illustrate specifically how these standards can be met.

Foundations of technology: Includes training in the basic operation of a computer, examining the acceptable use of a computer as a learning tool, and the understanding of vocabulary associated with the use of technology.

Use technology to acquire information: Students will be made aware of various productivity tools used to make their work easier, examine available electronic resources; use electronic research tools; and evaluate material for its relevancy to their needs.

Use technology to solve problems: Use of computer-based productivity tools to create and modify solutions to problems, use research skills and electronic communication to create new knowledge, use technology applications to evaluate the process and product of their work.

Use technology to communicate: Use of technology to practice and enhance communication skills; give practice in formatting digital information for effective communication; use computers to reach out to other parts of the community and the world to increase their knowledge; and design new products electronically using a variety of media.

Reprinted with permission from National Educational Technology Standards for Students (June, 1998), published by the International Society for Technology in Education (ISTE), NETS Project. The full document is available from ISTE at 800.336.5191 and at http://cnets.iste.org

Your computer is made up of many different hardware devices. The hardware consists of all the parts you can touch and see. All of the following are hardware devices:

- the system unit
- the disk and CD-ROM drives
- the keyboard
- the mouse
- the monitor
- the printer

Hardware can be defined as being input devices, output devices, or input/output devices (sometimes called **I/O devices**), depending on the direction the information flows between the device and the system unit. The disk and CD-ROM drives, keyboard, monitor, printer, and mouse are also called peripheral devices, since they plug into the system unit and support the operation of the computer.

The System Unit

This is the main controlling unit of your computer. The system unit is the actual computer. It is that large box that sits on the floor or on your desk.
It consists of the following components:

1. The CPU, which stands for the Central Processing Unit, controls the rest of your computer and processes all the data that goes through the machine. The CPU rests on an integrated circuit chip. This chip is the brain of your computer.
2. The memory that stores short-term data. There are two kinds of memory: RAM and ROM. The most important is Random Access Memory, or RAM. Before your CPU can process information and run programs, that information and those programs must be in RAM. As you may create a document using a word processor, that document stays in RAM memory until it is saved permanently to a disk drive. ROM stands for Read Only Memory and is a secondary memory that contains some system start-up instructions.
3. The power supply that ensures your computer gets enough continuous power to perform its computing tasks. Problems may arise with your computer if your power supply is erratic or inefficient.

Disk and CD-ROM Drives

The two kinds of disk drives are: hard disk drives, which are non-removable, fast and hold a lot of information; and floppy disk drives, which are slower than hard disks and do not hold as much information. The advantage of using removable diskettes in the floppy drives is to allow you to transfer and share data between two or more computers, or as a data backup for information you may not wish to lose in the event of inevitable computer failures. The term drive refers to the box in which you insert diskettes and CD-ROMs. Hard disk drives contain non-removable disk platters that hold data and programs.

The disk drives provide for extended long-term memory. When you turn off the computer, the data on the disks remains on the disks. The data leaves a disk drive only when you issue commands to remove that data. The contents of RAM disappears when you close a software program or turn off your computer.

The disks and RAM work together. When you need to run a program, such as a word processor, you'll tell the computer to load that program from a disk drive into RAM. Once it is loaded into RAM, your CPU can then execute the instructions in that program.

A CD-ROM drive holds compact disks that look like the audio CDs you have seen and listened to. A CD-ROM drive can hold over 600 megabytes of information. Although CD-ROMs operate more slowly than their hard disk counterpart, their capacity makes them almost a necessity in today's computers. Multimedia (the audio and video capabilities of computers) often requires the huge storage capacities of CD-ROM drives to hold motion video and sound.

The Keyboard

The keyboard of your computer works very much like a typewriter keyboard. Your keyboard also has a numeric keypad on the right side. You must first select **Num Lock** to activate the numeric keypad. The **Enter** key operates much the same as a carriage return on most typewriters. You use the Enter key at the end of a paragraph, instead of at the end of a line in a word processor, since most word processors incorporate word wrap that automatically brings the cursor to the beginning of a new line as you type. The **Caps Lock** key allows you to type in all capital letters. The use of the **Shift** key allows for single capital letters, such as the first word of a sentence.

In addition to Shift, there are these additional modifier keys: **Alt** and **Ctrl**. The Alt key (meaning alternative) and Ctrl (meaning control) give additional choices to your keyboard. Therefore, you can Press A, Shift-A, Alt-A, or Ctrl-A. Different programs use these modifier keys differently. For example, Alt-F might display a list of file options or select an item on the screen.

You'll find 10 or 12 keys labeled F1 through F10 (or F12). They are called **Function** keys. A function key often performs several tasks depending on what you're doing at the time. Each program that you run responds differently to the function keys. F1 is the key most often used to display a **Help** file in a program.

The **Escape** (Esc) key often lets you back up one step when working on your PC. For example, if you start to print a document you can often press Esc to cancel the printing. As with the function keys, each program that you run handles the Esc key differently.

There are always at least four keys with arrows on them. These are the **Cursor-directional** keys. A **cursor** is a blinking underscore, straight vertical line, or box that indicates where the next typed character will appear on the screen. Often you can move the cursor around the screen using various arrow keys.

Four additional cursor-movement keys, the **Home**, **End**, **PageUp**, and **PageDown** keys move the text cursor around on the screen. Each of these keys behaves differently depending on how the programs you run react to them. During the movement of the text cursor, you can often press the **Insert** (Ins) and **Delete** (Del) keys to change text already on the screen by inserting and deleting text.

Pointing Devices

Computers now come equipped with one of several types of pointing devices which allows you to perform actions with your computer that were once done with keyboard commands and the use of modifier and function keys. Most actions you do with a pointing device can also be done with keyboard commands, but the pointing device makes it so much easier! The most commonly used pointing device in today's computers is the **Mouse**. While it appears rather awkward the first time you use it, it is a lifesaver over trying to remember the keystrokes necessary to perform specific operations with your computer. Other devices are available, which may include a **Trackball**, **Wheel mouse**, or **Touchpad**. The wheel is designed for ease of scrolling through documents and Internet web pages. The trackball and touchpad are commonly attached to portable notebook systems, and are sometimes included with desktop systems. Each button or ball reacts much the same as a comparable button on a mouse.

How to Operate the Mouse

Move and point the mouse—You actually move the mouse across your desk. The screen's mouse cursor follows your movements.

Click—To "click the mouse," press and immediately release either the left or right mouse button. Screen objects are usually selected with the left button. A right button click usually displays a special pop-up menu. This action, new in Windows 95, provided the first use for the right mouse button.

Double-click—Press and release the mouse button twice quickly, usually to activate a program.

Drag—This function enables you to move certain items on the screen by highlighting or clicking on them. Used specifically for editing purposes, hold down your left mouse button, and move the selected object around on your screen.

To practice using the mouse, go to the Mouse icon in the control panel. There is a setting that will allow you to customize your single and double click speed. It will also allow you to reset the primary mouse button from left to right for a left-handed user.

Monitor

The **monitor** is the device that displays the results of your actions from within your computer. It would be impossible to operate a computer without one! Monitors come in a wide range of sizes. The standard size is 14–15 inches (measured diagonally), but displays are available as large as 21 inches. Price is adjusted accordingly—the larger the monitor, the more expensive it is. It also takes more of the system resources to operate a larger monitor display. Good quality monitors in the 17 to 21 inch range need a more powerful video card with at least 4 to 8 megabytes of video memory. They allow for more information to be displayed on the screen at one time in a higher resolution for ease of reading.

Printer

The **printer** is the device that allows you to get paper copies of information from within your computer. If you have no printer you must file your information on a floppy disk and take it to a computer (which has the same software program you created the file in) that has a printer attached. There are three types of printers: **laser**, **inkjet**, and **dot matrix**. They are discussed in detail later.

COMPUTER SYSTEMS

Every computer is made up of many components, called hardware. There are three main types of computer systems. Each of these systems has its advantages and disadvantages, depending upon the use for which the system is intended. Many times the choice depends upon the preference of the user or the amount of available desk space.

All computer systems, regardless of their style, include the following devices: the **central processing unit**, **short term memory** (RAM), **disk** and/or **CD-ROM drive**(s), **keyboard**, **mouse**, **monitor**, and a dependable power supply. Additional hardware devices that are desirable to connect to a computer include speakers, microphone, and a printer.

Desktop System

Desktop systems take up much less desk space than a tower system. If the area your computer will occupy is limited, this may be the system for you. It conveniently allows you to set the monitor atop the system unit, freeing up desk space for other devices attached to your computer. You are limited, however, to expansion space within the unit itself for future upgrades and additions to your system. Most often today, desktop systems are used as "workstations" in a network that pulls most of its files from the network "server".

Tower System

The advantage of owning a tower system is that it allows for more room inside the chassis for adding to your computer in the future. It does take up more space on the desk. If the space it will occupy is limited, you may want to consider a desktop system. Often, when short on space, tower systems may be placed on the floor to allow for more workspace on the desk.

Laptop or Notebook System

Laptop systems are wonderfully portable and an ideal choice for those who must work on the go. They tend to be much more expensive than the tower or desktop systems, for the comporable speed, and the display is much smaller. They are especially useful for their portability if you are a frequent user of presentation software. They operate on battery power, so there is not the problem of locating a power source when it is in use.

Network Server

A server is a large computer containing many files that may be shared over a network. A network is a group of computers that connect together for the purpose of communicating with each other and sharing information. The server is usually more powerful than the workstations that pull information from it.

PRINTER CHOICES

Dot Matrix Printer

Advantages of Use: inexpensive to operate, uses ribbon cassettes instead of ink; prints on multiple copies/carbons; fast output of printed material

Disadvantages of Use: noisy; needs special paper since it is pin-fed; tends to overheat when large amounts of printing are done; lower quality of text and graphics

Inkjet Printer

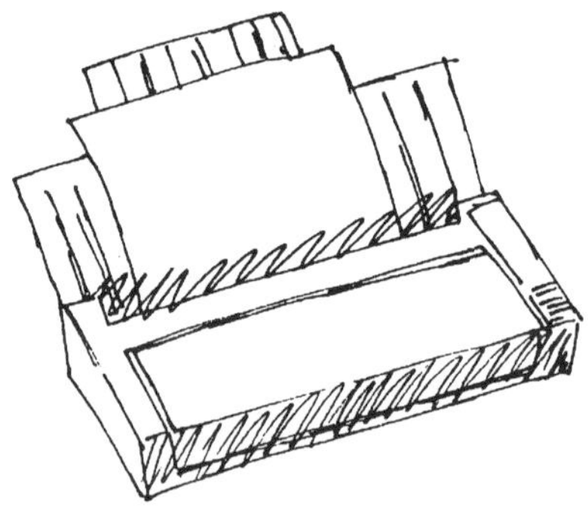

Advantages of Use: reasonably priced; prints in color; uses regular copy paper; good text and graphic output

Disadvantages of Use: expensive to maintain, especially when printing in color; slow output of material; best quality print when special paper is used

Laser Printer

Advantages of Use: fast output of material; uses regular copy paper; more easily configured for use over a network; excellent text and graphic output

Disadvantages of Use: expensive to purchase

Portable Printer

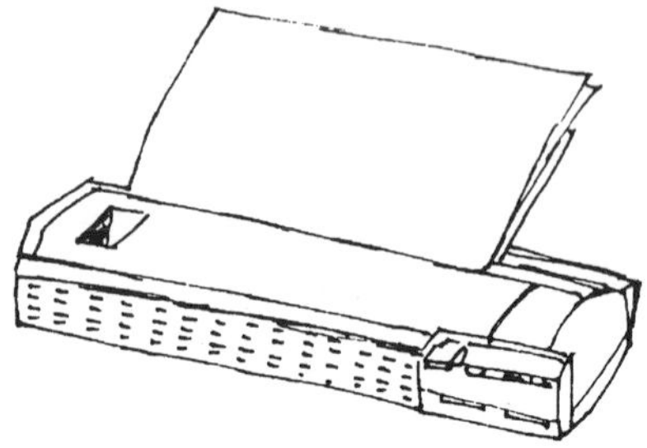

Advantages of Use: conveniently small and portable for use with a notebook system; uses regular copy paper

Disadvantages of Use: expensive to purchase and to maintain

USING A COMPUTER IN YOUR CLASSROOM

Many elementary schools do not yet have computer labs for students to use. It therefore becomes the responsibility of the classroom teacher to become proficient enough in its use to provide instruction in technology. The first step in implementing technology in your classroom is through the purchase and utilization of a **scan-converter**. This device allows you to connect the monitor of your computer to a television screen to facilitate a computer display the entire class can view. Scan converters can be purchased through computer hardware dealers. The quality level of the screen resolution displayed will determine the price.

There are many examples of software today that promote the use of technology in classrooms with a single computer. Interactive software that provides opportunities for problem solving in small groups is one choice. However, individual students can use math, reading, and other subject-related software for skills enhancement.

Internet access within your classroom opens your students to the world. It allows your classroom to participate in e-mail/keypal projects, Web Quests, and Internet Scavenger Hunts. The television screen can enable you to take your class on "Virtual Field Trips" to places you could never physically visit.

If a scan-converter is not feasible for you to purchase, you can still use your computer and Internet access to enhance your teaching materials. There are many free materials available for you to order, and lots of sites offer lesson plan ideas. Some examples of those sites include:

Alphabet™ Superhighway .... http://www.ash.udel.edu/ash

Busy Teachers Web Site K-12 .... http://www.ceismc.gatech.edu/busyt

Classroom Connect .... http://www.classroom.net

Cyberguides:
Teacher & Student Activities http://www.sdcoe.k12.ca.us/score/cy68.html

Discovery Channel School .... http://www.discoveryschool.com

Education World™ .... http://www.education-world.com

Gander Academy
Theme-Related Resources .... http://www.stemnet.nf.ca/CITE/themes.html

The Gateway to
Educational Materials (GEM)...... http://www.thegateway.org

The Lesson Plan Place .... http://www.inet-edu.com/lessons/index.html

Pacific Bell's Knowledge Network:
Blue Web'n.. http://www.kn.pacbell.com/wired/bluewebn

Multimedia Encyclopedias

The invention of the CD-ROM, and its inclusion in a computer system, opened an exciting new world of possibilities for educational materials. It allowed for full-motion video, sound, and animations to be played through the computer system without having to take up valuable hard drive space. At the time of the inception of the CD and the CD-ROM player, hard drives were minimal in size by today's standards. As hard drive capacity increased due to demands made by newer, more graphic-intense applications, the need for CD's has become a necessity.

The amount of information stored on one CD is equivalent to what had be stored on nearly 400 floppy disks formerly. This gives you some idea of the amount of information included in a multimedia encyclopedia. What used to take up a whole row of shelves in a home or school library is now contained in a small case on one or two CD's. Multimedia encyclopedias are much less expensive than hardbound volumes. They range in price from about $30 to $120. Updates are managed over the Internet, alleviating the need for annual yearbook supplements. Some companies offer a subscription plan that allows you to purchase a new edition of their encyclopedia yearly at a reduced cost. The following list is a sample of available multimedia encyclopedias. If you are interested in purchasing a multimedia encyclopedia for use at home or at school, check the company's web address for a complete overview of features, pricing, and ordering information. Look for a sampler of the product on the web site to get an idea of what you are getting before you buy.

Compton's Encyclopedia 99 Deluxe (Win 95/98)................. http://www.learningco.com
The Learning Company
One Athenaeum St.
Cambridge, MA 02477

Encarta Encyclopedia Deluxe 99 (Win 95/98)....................... http://www.microsoft.com
The Microsoft Corporation
One Microsoft Way
Redmond, WA 98052-6399

Britannica CD 99 Multimedia Edition (Win 95/98) .... http://www.eb.com
Encyclopaedia Britannica
Customer Service Department
310 S. Michigan Avenue
Chicago, IL 60604

1999 Grolier Multimedia Encyclopedia (Windows, Mac) .... http://www.grolier.com
Grolier Interactive, Inc.
90 Sherman Turnpike
Danbury, CT 06816

1999 World Book
Multimedia Encyclopedia (Windows, Mac) .... http://www.worldbook.com
World Book
525 West Monroe St., 20th Floor
Chicago, IL 60661

Search Engines and Subject Guides

The Internet is made up of millions of web sites containing information on almost any topic you can think of, and it is growing daily. Accessing the information you need is difficult if you don't know where to go to find it. It is like being in the world's largest library with no card catalog to find what you're looking for. The Internet tools that helps you get the information you are pursuing are **search engines. Lycos** (http://www.lycos.com) and **Yahoo!** (http://www.yahoo.com) are two of the most popular search engines. Search engines are helpful for browsing general information and for finding specific resources. A search engine indexes information in several ways, most commonly by topic and source. There are many search engines available, and the one you use depends largely on the kind of information you are seeking. The search is done through keywords you initially provide. The search can be refined through the operative wording you choose. Many Internet service providers have a link to the various search engines on their home page, or you may access them directly through their web addresses.

There are many effective resources available online to help educators get started in doing a search; two are listed here. Kathy Schrock has several slide presentations online at her site: http://www.discoveryschool.com/schrockguide. Memphis City Schools' Teaching and Learning Academy has a step-by-step explanation of doing a search at http://www.memphis-schools.k12.tn.us/admin/tlapages/search.htm.

AltaVista .... http:// www.altavista.digital.com
This searches the entire Internet for HTML files. It is one of the largest and most extensive engines. It provides through an advanced search the opportunity to access Usenet newsgroups, which give the most current information on trends on the Internet.

Excite .... http://www.excite.com
Excite has an easy to use interface, which provides an option for "More Like This", once you have done a search. It also provides links to current weather and news for your particular area, and provides some reviews of other new sites.

HotBot .... http://www.hotbot.com
This site will sort the results by date or media type. It provides links to information pertinent to teachers searching educational information.

Infoseek .... http://www.infoseek.com
This engine enables you to search web sites, companies, news, and newsgroups. It offers a good tutorial in how to search and how to refine your search, through a link to Search Tips.

Lycos .... http://www.lycos.com
This is one of the oldest search tools on the Internet, but has managed to keep up-to-date with lots of options for searches available.

Northern Light .... http://www.northernlight.com
This is one of the newest available engines. Search over 100 Million Web pages and the trademarked Special Collection of 5000 full text sources. Your results are categorized into custom search folders to organize your results as you specify.

WebCrawler™ .... http://www.webcrawler.com
This is a good place to start if you are new to keyword searching. It is a good place for locating major web resources.

What is ERIC? (http://www.accesseric.org: 81)

The Educational Resources Information Center (ERIC) is a national information system designed to provide users with ready access to an extensive body of education-related literature. The U.S. Department of Education: Office of Educational Research and Improvement and the National Library of Education support ERIC, which was established in 1966. From the ERIC homepage you can access each of the sixteen ERIC Clearinghouses and the ten Adjunct Clearinghouses.

The ERIC Clearinghouses collect, abstract, and index education materials for the ERIC database, respond to requests for information in their subject specific areas, and produce special publications of current research, programs, and practices. Currently these sixteen clearinghouses cover a wide range of areas related to education. There are also ten adjunct clearinghouses whose focus may overlap one or more of the clearinghouses. An example: there is an ERIC Clearinghouse on Assessment and Evaluation which seeks to provide balanced information concerning education assessment and resources to encourage responsible test use. There is also an Adjunct Clearinghouse on Test Collection that gives descriptions of available assessment and evaluation tools.

ERIC provides expertise in all areas by drawing from resources across the country. Locations are in New York, Maryland, Virginia, West Virginia, Washington, D.C., North Carolina, Indiana, Ohio, Illinois, Oregon, and California. The ERIC Clearinghouse on Information and Technology at Syracuse University in New York offers wonderful resources for any teacher interested in integrating technology into their classroom. Some features found at this location follow.

AskERIC

Do you need to know the latest information on some topic in education or curriculum? Just AskERIC! When you submit your education question to the AskERIC Q&A, you'll receive a personal e-mail response from one of their information specialists within two business days. You will receive a list of ERIC database citations that deal with your topic. They will also refer you to other Internet resources for additional information.

Virtual Library

This section contains selected educational resources including:

1) AskERIC InfoGuides: Topical indices of frequently asked questions receive by AskERIC's Question and Answer Service. There is available a wealth of inforation on current trends in education.

2) AskERIC Lesson Plans: 1000+ submitted to AskERIC, plus links to other sources for lesson plans.

3) The AskERIC Toolbox: Internet resources used by the Network Information Specialists to answer education-related questions.

World Wide Web Projects

AskERIC works with several organizations, supporting their efforts in providing education information over the Internet. Some of the projects include:

The Teacher-Pathfinder Internet Village: This project, funded through a grant from the U.S. Department of Education, links teachers from all over the world into one community. The sites within the village include a community center, a schoolhouse, support offices, a parent building, and a professional development building.

Consortium for School Networking: A non-profit organization, it promotes the use of telecommunications in K-12 education to improve learning. Their main goals are to educate and inform policy makers of the value of K-12 networking, and ensure wise public policies affecting schools in cyberspace.

KidsConnect: KidsConnect is for students what AskERIC is for teachers. If Internet research is the wave of the future, we must provide children with the direction for research. Designed especially for school library media specialists, teachers, and students, it offers anyone the opportunity to learn the skills necessary to navigate the Information Super Highway. Students from kindergarten through grade 12 can submit a question they are researching. The Information Specialists will respond via e-mail within 2 school days. Since this is an Internet-based service, most often it will point you to Internet resources. Sometimes the information needed is in the school library. Students are encouraged to seek help from the school librarian in addition to sources found through KidsConnect.

Virtual Reference Desk: The goal of the Virtual Reference Desk project is to link the K-12 community, including students, teachers, and parents, to experts through digital reference. Digital reference is also known as "Ask-An-Expert" service. It provides the educational community with links to experts in technology, the arts, social studies, science, health, and physical education, to name a few. The Virtual Reference Desk does not actually answer questions, but provides resources and links to experts who offer these services. VRD seeks to place people in contact with people who can answer specific questions and instruct users on developing certain skills.

Gateway to Educational Materials (GEM): This database contains in excess of 3000 lesson plans for grades K-12 in all subject areas. It truly makes ERIC a lifesaver and a timesaver as well. Lots of ideas for integrating technology into your curriculum can be found here.

A TEACHER'S MAP OF THE INTERNET

The Internet has truly revolutionized the quest for information by students and teachers alike. However, it certainly takes some skill and practice to successfully navigate through the many avenues of "The Information Superhighway." As with our modern highways, there is always construction going on. Therefore, on your travels through the internet, you may find many interesting detours and some roads once traveled-closed. New sites are added daily, and others are moved or are no longer available. It is important to keep your list of favorite places current, and keep notes on sites you visit. It is easy to get lost on such a busy thoroughfare!

Suggested Online Resources for Teachers

Web 66 Project http://web66.coled.umn.edu/

Just as U.S. Highway Route 66 was a catalyst for Americana, the World Wide Web is a catalyst that will integrate the Internet into K-12 school curricula. The Web66 project is designed to facilitate the introduction of this technology into K-12 schools. The goals of this project are:

1. To help K-12 educators learn how to set up their own Internet servers.
2. To link K-12 web servers and the educators and students at those schools.
3. To help K-12 educators find and use K-12 appropriate resources on the web.

Mustang Project.. http://mustang.coled.umn.edu/

The University of Minnesota Mustang project is the vehicle for teachers to cruise down Web66 on the World Wide Web. Web66 teachers don't "surf the net." Surfers go back and forth over the same territory at the mercy of the waves and never really get anywhere. Web66 teachers cruise the web with the style of a '67 Mustang, deciding when to travel, which direction to travel, and how far to travel. Web66 teachers are in full control of their own destiny and can seek out the best educational destinations anywhere on the web.

The goals of this project are:

1. To give K12 educators a management model for integrating the World Wide Web into their curriculum.
2. To help K12 educators design and implement Internet projects for their curriculum and graduation standards.
3. To provide an on-line staff development program for teachers who wish to integrate the Internet into their classroom

The Mustang project is part of Web66, a cooperative project with Hillside Elementary and the University of Minnesota College of Education and Human Development with the Center for Applied Research and Educational Improvement.

This project is made possible by a grant from 3M.

Global SchoolNet Foundation —
Linking Kids Around the World! .... http://www.gsn.org/

You'll love this site if you want to:

- find and connect with other classroom teachers around the world
- find interesting and productive global collaborative learning projects for your own classroom
- build, advertise, and conduct your own original collaborative projects

Site a Day .... http://www.seidata.com/~scunning/SiteADay

Designed for teachers and students by Scott Cunningham at Ball State University in Muncie, Indiana, this site provides links for each day of the school year. The links are varied and provide an excellent starting point for students to explore the Internet.

The Internet Public Library .... http://www.ipl.org

This resource provides a ready reference to websites on virtually every subject.

AskEric: Education Information
with the Personal Touch .... http://ericir.syr.edu

Provides a question and answer service for teachers. E-mail your question, and ERIC network information specialists will research and respond with their search of ERIC resources, databases, and Internet resources.

Kathy Schrock's Guide for Educators .... http://discoveryschool.com/schrockguide

Includes a list of classified sites in the Internet found to be useful for enhancing curriculum and teacher professional growth. There is a selection of teacher training slide presentations. It is updated daily to keep the links current.

Teacher Pathfinder .... http://teacherpathfinder.org

This award-winning web site provides a wealth of information for teachers, including lesson plans, curriculum links, and links to schools around the world.

Virtual Schoolhouse .... http://metalab.unc.edu/Virtual/Lessons/crossroads

This link provides a wonderful resource for teachers to browse. It includes classrooms, an art room, a playground, and even a teacher's lounge. It is packed with ideas for how teachers can apply technology resources in every area of their classroom.

Crossroads: A K-16
American History Curriculum .... http://ericir.syr.edu/Virtual/Lessons/crossroads/

Designed with a grant through the Fund for the Improvement and Reform of Schools and Teaching (FIRST) of the U.S. Department of Education, its goal is to provide an integrated curriculum in American history. This curriculum is called Crossroads, and is composed of thirty-six units distributed among all grade levels from kindergarten through high school. It is organized into twelve historical periods, each covered by a unit at each of the grade levels. It also offers guidelines for college-level preservice social studies teachers.

Other Starting Points for Research and Information:

Library of Congress .... http://lcweb.loc.gov

This web site allows an offering of a small portion of the American historical collections, as well as a catalog of resources, text and images from major exhibitions, the THOMAS database of information of the U.S. Congress, and a learning page for K-12 students.

The Info Service .... http://info-s.com

Info Service includes nearly 50,000 links to areas of interest—from computer problems and their solution to games to full-length texts of books. It is an excellent place to begin a search, for if it is to be found on the Internet, it most certainly is linked to this site.

The Library Spot .... http://www.libraryspot.com

Includes links to libraries on the Internet, as well as book sites and reference materials.

Encyberpedia .... http://www.encyberpedia.com/ency.htm

This site includes an annotated listing of subject-oriented encyclopedias available on the Web.

Encyclopedia.Com .... http://www.encyclopedia.com

Encyclopedia.Com provides current information in all major fields of knowledge. More than 17,000 articles provide free, quick, and useful information. The basic articles are free, but they may contain links to materials from The Electric Library, for which a fee is charged for access.

Encyclopedia Smithsonian .... http://www.si.edu/resource/faq/start.htm

This resource is based on a compilation of frequently asked questions to provide guidance in finding the requested information on topics available through The Smithsonian Institution.

Free Internet Encyclopedia .... http://clever.net/cam/encyclopedia.html

Internet-accessible information on a variety of topics arranged in an encyclopedic manner.

Librarians' Index to the Internet .... http://sunsite.berkeley.edu/InternetIndex

A searchable, annotated subject directory of almost 3000 Internet resources chosen for their usefulness to the public library user's information needs.

Webliography:
A Guide to Internet Resources .... http://www.lib.lsu.edu/weblio.html

From LSU Virtual Library, a well-annotated hierarchical guide to resources available on the Internet, covering a broad range of topics.

SUGGESTED ONLINE RESOURCES FOR STUDENTS

KidsConnect .... http://www.ala.org/ICONN/AskKC.html
This site allows students (with an e-mail address) to submit questions to an information specialist concerning a project or paper the student is working on. The information specialist will respond in two business days with Internet resources and library resources that are pertinent to their topic. The student is encouraged to seek help from the school librarian in addition to KidsConnect.

History and Social Studies Sites

Learning About the Oregon Trail .... http://ukans.edu/kansas/seneca/oregon/mainpage.html
From St Louis, Missouri, to Oregon City, Oregon, the Oregon Trail carried thousands of pioneer families to the promised land on the western frontier. The Oregon Trail was much more than a pathway to the state of Oregon; it was the only practical corridor to the entire western United States. This web site provides many links to the history of the Oregon Trail. Within the links are actual photographs of the sites visited in the game. Also included are maps, trail diaries, fantastic facts, and a history of the California goldrush.
The game *Oregon Trail* provides an opportunity for students to learn about western expansion in the United States, as well as simulate their own adventure on The Trail.

Presidents of the United States .... http://fujisan.demon.co.uk/USPresidents/preslist.htm
This link provides information about all the Presidents of the U.S.

The White House .... http://www.whitehouse.gov/WH/kids/html/kidshome.html
This link to the White House allows students the opportunity to tour the White House with Socks the Cat as tour guide.

Fifty States .... http://www.50states.com.
Access the home page of each of the fifty of our United States. Learn about the state bird, state tree, state flower, state flag, car license plate, and state song.

Science Sites

Bill Nye the Science Guy's Nye Lab Online .... http://nyelabs.kcts.org
This web site provides online ideas for lab experiments and a search engine for science online. Search by Life Science, Physical Science, or Planetary Science.

The Yuckiest Site on the Internet .... http://www.nj.com/yucky/index.html
New Jersey Online brings kids "The best place for science information and fun." The site includes "A Day in the Life of Ralph the Roach."

University of Oklahoma—Tornado Site .... http://www.caps.ou.edu
This site includes information about tornadoes, with links to other sites concerning weather.

The Nine Planets: A Multimedia Tour of the Solar System by Bill Arnet .... http://www.seds.org/billa/tnp/nineplanets.html
View pictures, sounds, and other links to information about our solar system.

The Dinosaur Society .... http://edtech.kennesaw.edu/web/dinopage.html
Includes links such as an exhibit of the dinosaurs of Jurassic Park, Dinoart, Dinoartists, and Visit a Dig.

Dinosauria Online .... http://www.dinosauria.com
The goal of creator Jeff Poling is to give the reader a broad exposure to dinosaur science.

Dino Russ's Lair .... http://www.isgs.uiuc.edu/dinos/dinos_home.htm
Dinosaur art, digs, exhibits, software, and information.

The Ornithological Council .... http://www.nmnh.si.edu/BIRDNET/
The ornithological information source for any type of bird.

ESPECIALLY FOR PRIMARY GRADES

Little Explorers .... http://www.enchantedlearning.com
Surf the web easily with a picture dictionary with links to over 1000 educational activities and games. The Enchanted Learning homepage has online activities including links to dinosaur activities and jokes, information about birds, links to information about schools in Japan and Africa, and a link to learning about our 50 states.

Fun School .... http://www.funschool.com
Many interactive games in all subject areas for children Pre-K through sixth grade. This site requires a Java-enabled browser.

Kid's Education .... http://www.siec.k12.in.us/~west/sites/kided.htm
Links to everything from crafts to online storybooks.

Random House Publishers .... http://www.randomhouse.com/kids
Includes activities for several of the children's books that have made Random House famous. This site requires a Shockwave plug-in that can be downloaded from this site.

Technology Integration http://www.mtnbrook.k12.al.us/tech/tech.htm
Links by subject and grade level.

VIRTUAL FIELD TRIPS

A virtual field trip allows a teacher to guide students on field trips to places which would not be physically possible to visit. Wonderful experiences await teachers and students who explore the vast resources available through online exhibits in museums and aquaria from all over the world. These field trips are as close as a few keystrokes!

VISIT AN ONLINE AQUARIUM

The Florida Aquarium	http://www2.sptimes.com/aquarium/default.htm
Great Barrier Reef Aquarium	http://aquarium.gbrmpa.gov.au
Marine Science Center	http://www.hurricane.net/~ashelton/amsc.htm
The Seattle Aquarium	http://www.seattleaquarium.org
The Sonoran Sea Aquarium	http://www.tucson.com/sea/page2.html
The Tennessee Aquarium	http://www.tennis.org
The Toba Aquarium	http://www.aquarium.co.jp/welcome-e.html
Vancouver Aquarium	http://oceanlink.island.net/vanaqu.html
Waikiki Aquarium	http://www.mic.hawaii.edu/aquarium

LEARN ABOUT THE RAINFOREST

Walk in the Rainforest	http://www.pbs.org/tal/costa_rica/rainwalk.html
Rainforest Links	http://www.mobot.org/MOBOT/education/tropics
Rainforests	http://www.slc.k12.ut.us/webweavers/lindam/listrainforest1.html
What Rainforest?	http://www.msu.edu/user/stracha5/links.htm

VISIT AN ONLINE MUSEUM

American Museum of Natural History—A site for exploring natural history and biodiversity	http://www.amnh.org
The Computer Museum—Fascinating interactive computer and technology exhibits	http://www.tcm.org
Exploratorium—Hands on science museum in San Francisco offers online versions of some of their current exhibits	http://www.exploratorium.edu
Field Museum of Natural History—Located in Chicago, this site is concerned with relationships in nature and among cultures	http://www.fmnh.org
Hands On Children's Museum—Online exhibits and interactivities	http://www.hocm.org
Imagination Station Science Museum	http://museums.mdmi.com/imaginationstation
Kennedy Space Center	http://www.spaceportusa.com/main.html
Museum of Science—Boston	http://www.mos.org
National Air and Space Museum—Online guide to galleries and exhibitions	http://www.nasm.si.edu
National Archives Online Exhibit Hall—Rotating virtual exhibits on U.S. History	http://www.nara.gov/exhall
Prehistoric Museum, College of Eastern Utah	http://www.ceu.edu/museum/museum.htm
The Smithsonian Institution—Directory to all the galleries and resources at the Smithsonian	http://www.si.edu
Wilbur R. Enns Entomology Museum	http://www.museum.insecta.missouri.edu

VISIT AN ONLINE ZOO

Audubon Zoo—New Orleans, featuring "The Interactive Swamp"	http://www.auduboninstitute.org
Los Angeles Zoo	http://www.lazoo.org
National Zoo—Washington, D.C.—Take the audio/video tour about the interdependency of plants and animals	http://www.si.edu/natzoo
San Diego Zoo	http://www.sandiegozoo.org
Woodland Park Zoo—Seattle, WA	http://www.zoo.org

In the interest of helping teachers to use computers in the most effective way possible, lesson plans are provided for incorporating the use of a computer with specific curriculum area objectives. These lesson plans are aimed not only at familiarizing students with computers, but also to provide advancement toward fundamental educational goals.

The curriculum areas explored include: Intelectual, Language, Physical, and Social Development, as well as Reading, Mathematics, and Science. The activities for each curriculum area are arranged in increasing levels of difficulty from level one to level six skills. Kindergarten students should likely begin with level one skills, while a third grade class may be more comfortable with level three skills. Teachers should assess the maturity level of students and their familiarity with computers before choosing the appropriate level of skills to implement in their classroom.

LESSON PLANS FOR LEVEL ONE SKILLS

Curriculum Area	Activity	Objective
Intellectual Development: Recognition of letters and numbers	Explore the use of the keyboard.	Identify input and output devices in the microcomputer system using specific keys with results noted on monitor: space bar, enter or return, arrow keys, letter, numbers, numeric keypad.
Social Development: Practices self-control, identifies and follows rules	Class develops rules for using the computer: follows directions for starting/ shutting down the computer, and entering/exiting a program.	Demonstrate proper care of computer equipment: both hardware and software, including proper sequence of turning equipment on and off.
Intellectual Development: Pattern recognition and repetition	Using Paint and a projection device, teacher demonstrates making a pattern and then tells students to copy it. Students will then practice the extension of the pattern.	Recognize that a computer requires instructions in order to operate effectively .
Intellectual Development: Speaks in complete sentences **Language Development**: Recognizes and repeats rhymes	Uses the sound recorder to record and play back voice speaking in complete sentences. Record and play back reciting of nursery rhymes.	Uses voice/sound recorder.

Curriculum Area	Activity	Objective
Intellectual Development: Work Habits	Whole class demonstration of CD-ROM: care and uses.	Student will be made aware of some of the different uses of the CD-ROM device with various software available, including games, encyclopedias, and dictionaries.
Physical Development: Small muscle control **Intellectual Development**: Recognition of letters and numbers	Introduction to use of grade-level appropriate typing program.	Student is made aware of proper keyboarding techniques such as correct hand and body positions and smooth and rhythmic keystroke patterns as grade-level appropriate.
Social Growth: Work habits, following directions	Class discussion on the importance of following rules as they apply to the use of computer programs.	Follow acceptable use policies when using computers.
Social Development: Respect for others **Intellectual Development**: Recognize that the work of others is not to be copied, whether it is classwork or work designed for use on a computer	Class discussion of terms, including licensing and copyright on grade-appropriate level.	Model respect of intellectual property by not illegally copying software or another person's electronic work.
Intellectual Development: Follow directions **Physical Development**: Small muscle control	Practice use of mouse. Use icons to open a program and menus to close a program.	Gain proficiency in the use of a mouse through following directions in a menu-driven program.
Intellectual Development: Work habits	Use of FILE and EXIT in a variety of programs to practice and enhance strategies for accessing programs.	Select appropriate strategies to acquire and access information.
Social Development: Tries new things	Use Paint to have children use the scissors tool to cut and paste something they have drawn to make a new picture.	Exposure to the concept of cut and paste using the computer.

Curriculum Area	Activity	Objective
Intellectual Development: Follows directions **Social development**: Tries new things; work habits	Students will exhibit an understanding of computer use by successfully entering and exiting grade-appropriate software, using grade-appropriate keyboarding skills.	Student evaluates to determine usefulness and appropriateness of digital information.
Intellectual Development: Application of learning **Social Development**: Work habits	Students will exhibit grade-appropriate success through interaction with grade-appropriate software and computer activities.	Student connects computer use to academic success and progress.
Intellectual development: Concept development, oral language skills, thinking skills	Interact with a variety of software to practice problem-solving techniques, including comparing, predicting, and drawing conclusions.	Choose and order the specific steps to the solution of a problem.
Intellectual Development: Concept development, oral language development, thinking skills, reference and study skills	Develop emerging use of encyclopedia, including maps and graphs, Internet, etc. to identify information needed to solve a variety of problems.	Use multimedia software programs to enhance learning experiences.
Intellectual Development: Concept development, oral language development, vocabulary development, alphabet recognition, beginning ABC order	Apply use of grade-appropriate encyclopedias and dictionaries to problem-solving situations.	Use appropriate software, including the use of multimedia to express ideas and solve problems.
Physical Development: Small muscle control **Intellectual Development**: Oral language, following directions	Locate and use a word processing program to practice emerging keyboarding skills. Practice keyboarding skills by typing with a grade-appropriate software program.	Recognize word-processing program as a tool for writing.
Intellectual development: Analysis, synthesis **Science**: Exploring animals	Practice using a dictionary and/or encyclopedia to identify groups of animals. Use body covering (hair, feathers, scales) as clues to groups.	Use electronic skills to build a knowledge base.

Curriculum Area	Activity	Objective
Intellectual Development: Evaluation, synthesizing, and categorizing **Social Development**: Working together, following directions	Use copy and paste features to copy pictures and captions into word processor to make class book about animals. Examples for sources might include electronic encyclopedias, dictionaries, and related clip art.	Use software features to evaluate work progress.
Intellectual development: Order steps to complete a task **Social Development**: Participate in activity	Use printing command to print out information about a specific animal.	Use of software and hardware features to evaluate final product.
Intellectual Development: Work habits	Whole class demonstration of the introduction to the Internet: connect with Enchanted Learning web site to learn about hyperlinks; communicate by E-mail with a known person outside of the school. www.enchantedlearning.com	Use communication tools to participate in group projects.
Physical Development: Small muscle control **Intellectual Development**: Recognition of colors and shapes, create personally meaningful writing	Use Paint to make pictures. Make a class Color Book and Shape Book with each child contributing a page illustrating a color word and shape.	Use electronic tools and computer skills to build a knowledge base regarding a topic, task or assignment.
Intellectual Development: Following directions	Child uses FILE menu to print shape and/or shape project. Child uses FILE menu and follows directions to save a file to floppy and/or hard disk. Student will then reopen file from saved location.	Demonstrates ability to publish information using a variety of media including monitor displays and printed materials at grade-appropriate level. Demonstrates ability to publish information using stored files.

Curriculum Area	Activity	Objective
Intellectual Development: Recognition of letters/numbers, writing name **Social development**: Following directions	Use Word Pad for writing activity to make a sign for child's room at home.	Use font attributes, color, and graphics to edit output information at grade-appropriate level.
Intellectual Development: Recognition of letters/ numbers, spelling readiness, beginning proofreading	Child evaluates sign for correct spelling, visual appeal, ease of readability of font selection.	Use font attributes, color, and graphics to ensure that products are suitable for communications media, including multimedia screen displays and printed materials with grade-appropriate success.
Social Development: Acquiring work habits	Class lesson with discussion of computer terms, followed by hands-on practice with the computer.	Identify and name the parts of the computer: monitor, CPU (brain), system unit, disk drive, mouse, keyboard, and speakers.
Intellectual Development: Vocabulary	Whole class discussion and demonstration. Talk about words that are unique to computers.	Have an understanding appropriate to their development of technology terminology: input, output, data, cut, copy, paste, drive, disk, desktop, menu.

LESSON PLANS FOR LEVEL TWO SKILLS

Curriculum Area	Activity	Objective
Language: Follow directions, participate in a discussion	Class lesson on Computer Basics followed by class discussion.	Review: parts of a computer, care of diskettes
Language: Follow directions, participate in a discussion, vocabulary development	Whole class discussion and demonstration. Paint: create a picture using cut and paste.	Understand and experience how a computer works: Input—You speak with a keyboard or mouse. Output—it responds with a monitor, sound, or the printer. Memory—it remembers what you tell it by screen display (short term) or on a hard drive or diskette (long term). Practice concept of cutting and pasting
Reading: Constructing meaning, left to right directionality, spaces between words, differences between whole words and letters **Language**: Writing/Mechanics—sentences and proper nouns begin with capital letters	Use of word processor or desktop publishing program to construct sentences.	Use of Caps Lock and Shift keys
Social Growth: Uses self-control, follows rules	Enters classroom quietly, listens to directions; follows directions for starting/shutting down computer and entering/exiting a program.	Demonstrates proper care of computer equipment; both hardware and software, including sequence of turning equipment on and off.
Language: Writing and composing	Use Paint to make a card for someone. Make a name sign, create letterhead, write a book report, compose a story.	Making capital letters (shift and caps lock), use keyboard with two hands, begin learning location of letters on keyboard; use space bar, return or enter, arrow keys

Curriculum Area	Activity	Objective
Language: Writing and composing, applying editing features to documents, use of correct mechanics in writing projects	Each child makes a page for a class book. Use correct mechanics in sentence construction; teacher specifies number of sentences to include.	Use of different kinds of fonts, printing, use of double and single spacing, use of graphics in documents.
Mathematics: Identifies and continues a pattern	Use Paint to make a pattern; let partner continue the pattern; introduce Solitaire	Manipulation of the mouse, locating a program from a menu, starting and ending a program, use of arrow keys and space bar, navigating through the computer.
Social Growth: Work habits, following directions	Class discussion on the importance of following rules as they apply to the use of computer programs.	Follow acceptable use policies when using computers.
Government/Citizenship: Respect for the work of others; recognize the work of others is not to be copied; use respect when operating a computer, so as not to harm the machine	Class discussion of terms, including licensing and copyright on grade-appropriate level.	Model respect of intellectual property by not illegally copying software or another person's electronic work; practice care in use of disks and computers.
Reading: Uses stories and books; literature appreciation	Practice use of mouse. Use icons to open a program and menus to close a program. Apply knowledge to use of a selection of electronic storybook software.	Gain proficiency in the use of a mouse through following directions in a menu-driven program; small group or individual activity in lab, which may be continued in classroom.
Science: Dinosaurs	Use software such as "Dinosaur Hunter" to learn about dinosaurs, including its linked web site: www.dkonline.com	Select appropriate strategies to acquire and access information; exposure to web browser and the Internet.
Reading: Writing and composing	Search for information about dinosaurs in a multimedia encyclopedia; use Paint to illustrate one of the dinosaurs they have studied.	Use of knowledge gained to express understanding of concepts.

Curriculum Area	Activity	Objective
Intellectual Development: Follows directions **Social Development**: Tries new things; work habits	Students will exhibit an understanding of computer use by successfully entering and exiting grade-appropriate software, using developing keyboarding skills.	Student evaluates to determine success of strategies used to acquire electronic information.
Reading: Uses stories and books	Students will practice and apply reading skills and computer skills using a selection of electronic storybook software.	Students further develop reading skills.
Intellectual Development: Application of learning **Social Development**: Work habits	Students will exhibit developmental success through interaction with grade-appropriate software and computer activities.	Student evaluates to determine usefulness and appropriateness of digital information.
Intellectual Development: Application of learning **Health**: The Human Body	Students will use Magic School Bus and the Human Body and a multimedia encyclopedia to look up pictures and study facts about the body.	Students will learn functions of the human body while learning about computer functions.
Intellectual Development: Concept development, oral language skills, thinking skills **Math**: Geometry and measurement—drawing two-dimensional shapes	Interact with a variety of software to practice problem-solving skills, including drawing shapes with Paint.	Choose and order the specific steps to the solution of a problem.
Intellectual Development: Concept development, thinking skills **Math Concepts**: Identify and practice use of coins—penny, nickel, dime, quarter	Develop emerging use of software programs to aide in development of formative concepts of money value.	Use multimedia software programs to enhance learning experiences.
Intellectual Development: Concept development **Math Concepts**: Telling time	Develop emerging use of software programs to aide in development of formative concepts of telling time.	Use appropriate software, including the use of multimedia to express ideas and solve problems.

Curriculum Area	Activity	Objective
Intellectual Development: Concept development **Math Concepts**: Math facts	Class discussion with grade-appropriate applications to give practice in computation skills, including appropriate software programs.	Use of multimedia software programs to enhance learning and apply problem-solving strategies.
Intellectual Development: Oral language, following directions **Computer Basics**: Developing keyboarding skills	Locate and use a word processing program to practice beginning keyboarding skills. Practice keyboarding skills by typing with a grade-appropriate software program.	Recognize a word-processing program as a tool for writing.
Intellectual Development: Analysis, synthesis **Science/Math Development**: Balancing and weighing	Use a desktop publishing program to create a document with two columns. Label the columns Light and Heavy. Use the picture frame tool to insert pictures matching the labels into each column.	Use electronic skills to build a knowledge base.
Intellectual Development: Evaluation, synthesizing, categorizing **Social Development**: Working together, following directions **Science**: Plants	Paint: draw pictures to illustrate the life cycle of a plant. Use a desktop publishing program to write about each of the stages of plant growth. Look up and view the short film of a germinating seed in a multimedia encyclopedia.	Use software features to evaluate work progress.
Intellectual Development: Order steps to complete a task **Scientific Investigations**: Insects **Social Development**: Participates in activity	Use multimedia encyclopedia to look up pictures and information about insects. Visit the Cockroach web site. www.nj.com/yucky/index.html. Make a class insect book. Use printing command to print out information about a specific insect.	Use telecommunications to evaluate work progress.
Geography: Landforms, map-reading	View maps in multimedia encyclopedia, talk about landforms on a relief map. Use of multimedia software programs to enhance learning and apply problem-solving skills.	Exposure to computer research; use of alphabetical order of listings to find information.

Curriculum Area	Activity	Objective
Intellectual Development: Work habits **Computer Basics**: Use of features of computers and related software including copy and paste, word processor, and multimedia encyclopedia **Science**: Animals **Science**: Dinosaurs	Whole class demonstration of the Internet. Find and print pictures of animals for class Animal Book. Visit a zoo web site before going on a field trip to a zoo; visit a dinosaur web site such as: www.zoomdinosaurs.com	Use communication tools to participate in group projects.
Reading/Language Arts: Given a topic, the student will compose a simple story **Social development**: Follow directions, work together	Use Word Pad for writing activity to make a book of stories written by the student. Make covers for book to be given to someone as a gift.	Use font attributes, color, and graphics to edit output information at developmental level for a defined audience (family). Use the computer to produce items of value.
Intellectual development: Recognition of letters/numbers, spelling readiness, beginning proofreading **Language arts/composition**: Writing an invitation	Students from upper grade classes team up with younger students to help them compose and write an invitation to a class activity. Older partners type invitation and save it. Working with it, they illustrate it with computer graphics.	Use font attributes, color, and graphics to ensure that products are suitable for communications media, including multimedia screen displays and printed materials: grade-appropriate level of success.
Social development: Follow directions, work together in group activity	"Buddies" from upper grades meet with younger students for cooperative computer learning. Use of desktop publishing program and word processor will be emphasized.	Demonstrates ability to publish information using a variety of media including monitor displays and printed materials as developmentally appropriate.
History: Comparing methods of communication of long ago and today	Find an older person to e-mail. Make a list of questions to be answered concerning the changes they have seen in their lifetime. Have the person come to class to meet and discuss questions. Use the encyclopedia to research the history of communications.	Exposure to various types of telecommunication.

LEVEL THREE SKILLS

Curriculum Area	Activity	Objective
Language: Follow directions, participate in a discussion	Whole class lesson on computer basics followed by class discussion.	Review the parts of a computer, care of computer and diskettes.
Language: Follow directions, participate in a discussion, vocabulary development	Whole class discussion and demonstration, followed by monitored practice.	Understand and experience how a computer works: appropriate care and use of a computer; become familiar with terms describing operation of a computer (input, output, memory).
Reading and Language Arts: Writing, composing, and spelling	Use basic word processor to write sentences using spelling words.	Use of Caps Lock, Shift Keys, and Spacebar.
Language: Writing and composing—apply editing features to documents, using correct mechanics in writing projects	Use desktop publishing to write short illustrated reports; type short poems or haiku written in class.	Making capital letters (shift and caps lock); practice beginning keyboarding skills: use two hands, proper hand placement, begin learning location of letters on keyboard; use space bar, return or enter, and arrow keys.
Language and Art: Writing and illustrating	Write sentences on a recent class event or story. The teacher would set guides such as: type your name, write 4 sentences, use capital letters and punctuation. Illustrate story using Paint program.	Use computer for word processing, use of different fonts, double and single spacing, use of graphics in documents, cursor location and movement, exposure to spell check and saving and retrieving work.
Language: Writing, composing, expression, letter writing skills	Write an invitation, letter to Santa, practice spelling words, write a note to a friend; use font size and color to show meaning in descriptive writing.	Use of mouse, locating a program from a menu, starting and ending a program, use of arrow keys and spacebar, saving and retrieving work.

Curriculum Area	Activity	Objective
Social Studies: Government/Citizenship—Democratic decision-making, respect for others and environment	Make a class rule book for computer use with one or more rules contributed by each student.	Follow acceptable use policies when using computers, as well as conduct in daily life.
Economics: Supply and demand, wants and needs	Discuss economic principles as they apply to availability of materials in class; make a two-column paper showing on one side wants and on the other side needs.	Practice care in use of machines and supplies; use of software features to format document into columns.
Language Arts: Constructing meaning	Use multimedia encyclopedia to look up topics from class curriculum and read about them. (animals, states, etc.)	Introduction to electronic reference materials.
Science: Life cycles of animals	Use related web sites on the Internet to find information; explore encyclopedia for animations and video.	Select appropriate strategies to acquire and access information; exposure to web browser.
Reading: Writing and composing	Use Paint to have children illustrate one of the animals they have studied.	Use of knowledge gained to express understanding of concepts.
Science: Weather	Visit the weather web site at the University of Oklahoma. Use e-mail to share weather information with other areas of the country. wwwcaps.ou.edu	Use of Internet to gain information. Student evaluates to determine success of strategies to acquire electronic information.
Science: Habitats	Visit an online zoo to observe different habitats. Find and print information to make animal reports.	Student evaluates to determine usefulness and appropriateness of digital information.
Reading: Uses stories and books	Students will practice and apply reading skills and computer skills using a selection of electronic storybooks.	Student evaluates ability to read fiction on the computer.

Curriculum Area	Activity	Objective
Intellectual Development: Application of learning **Health**: The Human Body	Student will use Magic School Bus and the Human Body and a multimedia encyclopedia to look up pictures and study facts. Make a report on one of the body's systems.	Student evaluates to determine usefulness and appropriateness of digital information.
Intellectual Development: Concept development, oral language skills, thinking skills **Math**: Geometry and measurement—drawing shapes	Interact with a variety of software to practice problem-solving techniques, including drawing shapes with Paint.	Choose and order the specific steps to the solution of a problem.
Intellectual Development: Concept development, thinking skills **Math Concepts**: Identify and practice use of coins—penny, nickel, dime, quarter, half-dollar, making change	Develop emerging use of software programs to aide in development of emerging concepts of money value.	Use multimedia software programs to enhance learning experiences and to solve problems.
Intellectual Development: Concept development **Math Concepts**: Telling time	Develop emerging use of software programs to aide in development of emerging concept of telling time to the hour, half hour and quarter hour.	Use appropriate software, including the use of multimedia to express ideas and solve problems.
Math Concepts: Geometry and measurement, symmetry	Use Paint to write and illustrate fractions. Draw ½ of a shape and copy, paste, and flip it to make a complete object.	Manipulation of mouse, use of different tools within a software program.
Social Studies: Learn about the 50 states, map-reading, using directions on a map	Use search engine to find web sites for various states. Print map of state from multimedia encyclopedia; look up information on the state seal, flower, bird. www.50states.com	Research with the computer; exposure to applying search engine to do research through the Internet.

Curriculum Area	Activity	Objective
Intellectual Development: Analysis, synthesis **Science/Math Concepts**: Balancing and weighing, estimating	Use desktop publishing program to format a document with two columns. Label the columns light and heavy. Put pictures illustrating the labels into each column; insert approximate weight of each item beside its picture.	Use electronic skills to build a knowledge base; manipulate graphics to give meaning to a document.
Intellectual Development: Evaluation, classification, synthesis	Use Paint to draw a picture of the life cycle of a plant; write about each of the stages of plant growth.	Develop student artistic skills.
Intellectual Development: Order steps to complete a task **Science**: Birds **Social Skills**: Participates in group activity	Use encyclopedia to find pictures and facts about birds. Look for web sites about birds. www.nmnh.si.edu/BIRDNET Make class bird book. Use printing command to print information. Search multimedia encyclopedia for pictures of birds and their sounds.	Use software features to evaluate final product.
Geography: Landforms, map reading; compare natural/man-made features	View maps in multimedia encyclopedia; talk about how landforms are shown on a relief map. View a CD atlas as a class to talk about relief maps.	Exposure to computer-based research.
Language Arts: Written expression; creates personally meaningful writing **Health**: Self esteem—recognize that all people have feelings	Make a feelings book, with stories about different feelings.	Use communication tools to participate in group projects.
Computer Basics: Use of features of computer including copy and paste, word processor, multimedia encyclopedia, Internet	Use multimedia encyclopedia to look up different types of geological forms; whole class demonstration of the Internet; learn about volcanoes at "Volcano World". http://volcano.und.nodak.edu/vw.html	Use electronic tools and computer skills to build a knowledge base regarding a topic, task, or assignment.

Curriculum Area	Activity	Objective
Math: Data analysis and problem solving; operations and place value	Solitaire—application of problem-solving strategies. Math computation software: work on basic math facts. Type and print problems for a partner to complete.	Correct use of a computer by entering and exiting a program; use the menu to change options for cards and style of play; use of numeric keypad.
Reading/Writing: Given a topic, the student will compose a simple story	Use word processor for writing activity to make a book of stories written by student.	Use font attributes, color, and graphics to edit output information at grade-appropriate level.
Language Arts: Grade-appropriate reading, spelling, beginning proofreading **Writing/Composing**: Write an invitation	Each class member composes an invitation to parents for a special class activity.	Use font attributes, color, and graphics to ensure that products are suitable for communications media, including multimedia screen displays and printed materials: grade-appropriate level of success.
Intellectual Development: Follow directions, work together	Partners from upper grades meet together with younger students for a day of exploration of the computer. Second grader benefits from the experience of the older student, working with various publishing methods one-on-one.	Student demonstrates the ability to publish information using a variety of media, including monitor displays and printed materials at grade appropriate level.
History: Introduction to a timeline; compare and contrast people long ago and today	Make connection by e-mail to an elderly person willing to share experiences and answer questions. Look up Christopher Columbus in the multimedia encyclopedia. View a timeline in a multimedia encyclopedia—determine important events which have occurred since student was born.	Exposure to electronic communication.

LEVEL FOUR SKILLS

Curriculum Area	Activity	Objective
Oral Language/Vocabulary: Participate in a discussion **Computer Basics**: Build a knowledge base of computer terms	Whole class lesson followed by discussion.	Use appropriate technology terminology. Identify uses of technology and how it has changed people's lives. Identify and describe the characteristics of digital input, processing, and output.
Writing/Composing: Create a grade-appropriate report on a given topic	Use multimedia encyclopedia and word processor to copy and paste information for a report. Print the report.	Save and delete files, use menu options and commands, work with more than one software application (multi-tasking); identify telecommunications technologies used to locate information; access remote equipment on a network, such as a printer or other peripheral.
Citizenship: Follow directions; demonstrate care and respect in use of computer equipment	Use a variety of games (ex. Solitaire, Minesweeper®) to practice use of mouse, video display; practice use of devices to involve a variety of tasks: record voice and play back, use word processor, demonstrate proper care of devices.	Use input devices such as mouse, keyboard, disk drive, modem, voice/sound recorder, scanner, digital video, CD-ROM; identify technology tools used to collect, analyze, and display data.
Computer Basics: Develop keyboarding proficiency to include practice in spelling, writing and composing, and word processing skills.	Use selected keyboarding software program for instruction. Practice should support curriculum goals in language arts, spelling, and other subjects where applicable. 6-8 weeks of intensive keyboarding lessons should be followed by a short review of skills at the beginning of class all year long.	Use proper keyboarding techniques, such as correct hand/body position and smooth and rhythmic keystroke pattern. Demonstrate touch keyboarding techniques for operating the alphabetic, numeric, punctuation, and symbol keys at grade level. Demonstrate an appropriate speed on short timed exercises at suitable grade level skill.

Curriculum Area	Activity	Objective
Language Arts: Constructing meaning, writing/composing	Use computer for writing projects: holiday stories, class reports and newsletter, friendly letters, than you notes, invitations; bring in writing composed in classroom to edit, write sentences with spelling words.	Produce documents at keyboard, proofread, correct errors; use language skills, including capitalization, punctuation, and symbol keys as grade-level appropriate.
Social Studies: Government/Citizenship—decision making; respect for others and environment	Make a rule book for computer class with one or more rules contributed by each student.	Follow acceptable use policies when using computers, as well as conduct in daily life. Recognize the Copyright Law protects what a person, group, or company has created.
Economics: Supply/demand, care of use of materials in computer lab; wants/needs	Discuss economic principles as they apply to materials in computer lab; make a two-column paper showing wants and needs.	Practice care in use of disks, computers, and supplies; use of software features to format document into columns.
Science: Space, sound	Visit Nine Planets web site to view planets and stars. Look up facts on planets and stars in multimedia encyclopedia. Choose a constellation and draw a picture of it using Paint. Make a class book. www.seds.org/billa/tnp/nineplanets.html Use the voice/sound recorder to record voice and observe soundwave graph in playback.	Acquire information including text, audio, video, and graphics. Apply critical analysis to resolve information conflicts and validate information.
Computer Basics: Build a knowledge base	Explore the use of online help by reviewing start menu. Take Windows Tour: explain and practice use of online help through "Tricks & Tips" and "Help" in the Start Menu.	Use online help and documentation.

Curriculum Area	Activity	Objective
Social Studies: Geography	Use the atlas in a multimedia encyclopedia to note cardinal directions and legend. Print a map of your state and locate your town.	Determine success of strategies used to acquire electronic information.
Social Studies: Government/citizenship	Class discussion on levels of government; take the Kid's Tour of the White House on the Internet. Use Paint to make a graphic representation of something learned. www.whitehouse.gov/WH/kids/html/kidshome.html	Determine usefulness and appropriateness of digital information.
Language Arts: Locating information	Use multimedia encyclopedia to find information on the ocean and coral reef.	Use software programs with audio, video, and graphics to enhance learning.
Science: Ocean Life **Math**: Graphing	Continue research about the ocean through the Internet. Visit an online aquarium. Combine research to make a report about an ocean animal. Make a spreadsheet graph of ocean animals with criteria such as size, location, and depth.	Use appropriate software to express ideas and solve problems including use of word processing, graphics, databases, spreadsheets, simulations, and multimedia. Use a variety of data types including text, graphic digital audio, and video.
Health: Nutrition **Math**: Graphing	Learn about good nutrition. Make a graph of food you ate yesterday by food group. Design a healthy menu.	Use communication tools to participate in group projects.
Social Studies: American History	Play "Oregon Trail" in groups of 4. Keep online journal of trip. Visit the Oregon Trail web site: http://ukans.edu/kansas/seneca/oregon/mainpage.html	Use interactive technology environments such as simulations, virtual museum field trips or online interactive lessons to manipulate information.
Social Studies: Community Awareness	Connect to your community via e-mail. Write to county officials and invite them to visit the class.	Participate with electronic communities as a learner, initiator, contributor, or mentor.

Curriculum Area	Activity	Objective
Music: Types of musical instruments	Sort pictures using Search feature to find pictures and articles in multimedia encyclopedia about musical instruments. Prepare a slide show presentation from sorted pictures and sounds.	Use software features to evaluate work progress. Use software features, such as slide show previews, to evaluate final product.
Health: Diseases; bacteria and viruses	Use interactive software such as Magic School Bus Explores the Human Body to search for what diseases do in the body and how germs make you sick. Search Internet for information on bacteria/ viruses; create a multimedia story as a class activity: how germs get into the body, how the body defends itself, what white blood cells do.	Use font attributes, color, and graphic to design products for a defined audience; evaluate finished product for appropriateness to the subject and audience.
Social Studies: Working together **Reading/Language Arts**: Writing/composing **Computer Basics**: Use and Care	Create a multimedia project as a group/class activity on "Care and Use of Computers".	Use presentation software to communicate with specific audiences.
Math: Charts and graphs	Identify the parts of a spreadsheet and what it is used for; use a spreadsheet to make a simple chart following written directions for the teacher. View the various types of graphs and charts that can be generated.	Use appropriate applications including spreadsheets and databases to develop charts and graphs by using data from various sources.
Language Arts: Writing/composing **Literature**: Style (newspaper article) **Art**: Graphic design—creation and manipulation of computer-generated graphics	Create a class newsletter as a group project. Select and/or design graphics to illustrate articles.	Publish information in a variety of media included printed copy, monitor display, documents, and video.

Curriculum Area	Activity	Objective
Language Arts: Writing/composing—students are given story starters to complete at selected times throughout the school year.	At the end of the 1st, 3rd, and 5th grading periods the student creates a project with the word processor and saves it on floppy disk for teacher to evaluate. Student meets with teacher for conference on progress.	Select representative products to be collected and stored for evaluation. Evaluate the product for relevance to the assignment or task.
Language Arts: writing/composing **History**: Sequence of events **Literature**: Style (autobiography)	Each child creates an outline of his life, using events important to him. He then composes an autobiography by applying word processing skills. The student may compose an e-mail message or letter to someone the child knows who may have had an influence on his life.	Create technology assessment tools to monitor progress of project such as checklists, timelines, or rubrics. Explore the importance of telecommunications in today's world.
Computer Basics: Inside a computer	Use an old computer for students to take apart and look inside. Identify the parts of the computer. If you do not have an old computer at your disposal, try to arrange a field trip to a local computer repair shop and ask a technician to share his or her knowledge of computer parts.	Apply critical analysis to resolve information conflicts and to validate information.

LEVEL FIVE SKILLS

Curriculum Area	Activity	Objective
Language: Vocabulary development; participate in a discussion **Computer Basics**: Build a knowledge base of computer terms and history	Whole class lesson followed by discussion.	Use appropriate technology terminology; identify uses of technology and how it has changed people's lives: become familiar with the history of technology development in our country; identify and describe the characteristics of digital input, processing, and output.
Language Arts: Writing/composing; constructing meaning	Use desktop publishing program to create a class report. Use resources from Internet and encyclopedia to copy and paste information; print the report.	Save and delete files, use menu options and commands, work with more than one application (multitasking); identify telecommunications technology used to locate information; identify the differences between networked and non-networked computers; access remote equipment, such as a printer or other peripheral, on a network.
Citizenship: Follow directions; demonstrate care and respect in use of computer equipment	Use different games and software to practice use of mouse and video display; use devices to practice various tasks: record voice and play back, use word processor, demonstrate proper care of CD-ROM and disks.	Use a variety of input devices such as mouse, disk drive, keyboard, modem, scanner, voice/sound recorder, digital video, CD-ROM; identify technology tools used to collect, analyze, and display data.
Computer Basics: Develop keyboarding proficiency through activities in spelling, writing/composing, and word processing	Use selected keyboarding software for instruction. Practice should support curriculum goals in language arts, spelling, and other subjects. 6–8 weeks of intensive keyboarding lessons should be followed by a short review of skills all year long.	Use correct hand/body position and smooth, rhythmic keystroke pattern; develop touch keyboarding skills for operating the alphabetic, numeric, punctuation, and symbol keys at grade level; demonstrate speed on short timed exercises.

Curriculum Area	Activity	Objective
Language Arts: Writing/composing; constructing meaning	Use computer for writing projects: holiday stories, class reports and newsletters, friendly letters, thank you notes, invitations; bring in writing topic and try to finish it in one session; write short stories with spelling words.	Produce documents at keyboard—proofread and correct errors; use language skills, including capitalization, punctuation, and symbol keys as appropriate for grade level.
Social Studies: Government/citizenship—democratic decision making; respect for others and environment	Make a rule book with several rules contributed by each student.	Follow acceptable use policies when using computers, Internet, and e-mail; recognize the Copyright Law protects what a person, group, or company has created.
Language Arts: Locating and organizing information—select and use appropriate references.	Students use multimedia encyclopedia to look up topics from class curriculum: animals, plants, stars, magnets.	Apply appropriate electronic search strategies in the acquisition of information.
Language Arts: Literary forms—biography, autobiography, fantasy, realistic fiction, adventure, folktales	Research in encyclopedia, use search engine to search Internet for online examples of different genres. Explore and experience which resources are useful for purpose.	Select appropriate strategies to navigate and access information on networks, using Internet and intranet for research and resource sharing.
Science: Ocean; ocean animals	Use selected software about the ocean; student will select an ocean animal to research and write about. Use encyclopedia to view information about the ocean habitat. Search Internet for information about environmental issues pertaining to the ocean.	Acquire information including text, audio, video, and graphics.
Computer Basics: Build a knowledge base	Review start menu; take the Windows tour; practice and use online help through "Tips & Tricks" and "Help".	Use on-line help and documentation.

Curriculum Area	Activity	Objective
Science: Vertebrate and invertebrate animals	Explore encyclopedia to classify animals as to type; search Internet for pictures of each type of animal; prepare a two-column sheet to display vertebrate and invertebrate animals.	Apply critical analysis to validate information.
Social Studies: Geography—rainforests	Identify characteristics of a rainforest; research in encyclopedia; search Internet to locate rainforests and become aware of environmental issues they face.	Determine success of strategies used to acquire electronic information.
Social Studies: Government/citizenship	Class discussion on levels of government; visit the White House on the Internet, and take the tour. Use Paint to make a graphic representation of something they have learned.	Determine usefulness and appropriateness of digital information.
Language Arts: Locating information **Social Studies**: Learn about your state	Use encyclopedia to find information on your state; search the Internet for your state; use various resources to write a report on your state—either a location or famous person.	Use software programs with audio, video, and graphics to enhance learning experiences.
Science: Classes of animals **Math**: Graphing	Continue research about animals through the Internet. Visit an online aquarium; combine research to make a report on a freshwater animal; make a graph to compare features of ocean and freshwater animals.	Use appropriate software to express ideas and solve problems including use of productivity tools, simulations, and multimedia; use a variety of data types including text, graphics, digital audio, and video.
Health: Nutrition	Take the "Nutrition Expedition" at http://fscn.che.umn.edu/NutrExp/default.html. It includes an Internet Scavenger Hunt for students.	Use communication tools to participate in group projects.

Curriculum Area	Activity	Objective
Social Studies: State history **Science**: Cave formation	Search the Internet for information on state history; visit an online zoo, museum, and/or aquarium that may be located within the state; research natural history areas such as caves; locate caves and find out how they were formed. Tour a Virtual Cave at www.goodearth.com/virtcave.html.	Use interactive technology environments such as simulations, electronic science and math labs, or online interactive lessons to manipulate information.
Social Studies: Communities; government	Use e-mail as a way to reach out and connect to your community from the school. Visit your state government web site; e-mail the governor.	Participate with electronic communities as a learner, initiator, contributor, or mentor.
Music: Composers **Computer Productivity**: spreadsheets	Learn about various musical composers using the multimedia encyclopedia; sort musical selections by composer, using the search feature; choose a composer to report on. View the Microsoft Works tutorial, noting the section on spreadsheets.	Use software features, such as online help, to evaluate work progress.
Music: Composers and their works	Prepare a slide show presentation from sorted pictures and sounds about composers and their musical works.	Use software features, such as slide show previews to evaluate final product.
Language Arts: Writing/composing; style—autobiography **History**: Sequence of events	Student creates a timeline of important events in his life; use these events to create an autobiography.	Use of timelines to monitor progression of time and events; use computer skills to save and retrieve work in progress.
Social Studies: Working together **Language Arts**: Writing/composing; literary style—autobiography	Create a multimedia presentation as a group/class to include an autobiographical slide each student has designed.	Use presentation software to communicate with specific audiences.

Curriculum Area	Activity	Objective
Social Studies: World regions—tundra, rainforest, desert **Science**: Animals **Math**: Charts and graphs	Explore Internet to find information on each region as it is studied. Identify the parts of a spreadsheet and discuss its use. Use a spreadsheet to make a simple chart of the characteristics of each region as it is studied; note plant and animal life of each region on spreadsheet; view the types of graphs that can be generated.	Use applications such as spreadsheets and databases to develop charts and graphs by using data from varied sources.
Language Arts: Writing/composing; style—newspaper article **Art**: graphic design—creation and manipulation of computer-generated graphics	Create a class newsletter as a group project; select and/or design graphics to illustrate articles; determine print setup—portrait or landscape—to print document; apply changes with print setup menu.	Publish information using a variety of media including printed copy and monitor display.
Language Arts: Writing/composing; students are given story starters to complete at selected times throughout the school year	At the end of the 1st, 3rd, and 5th grading periods, the student creates a project with the word processor and saves on floppy for teacher to evaluate; student meets with teacher for conference on progress.	Select representative products to be collected and stored in an electronic evaluation tool; evaluate the product for relevance to the assignment or task.

LEVEL SIX SKILLS

Curriculum Area	Activity	Objective
Language Arts: Vocabulary development; participate in a discussion **Computer Basics**: Build a knowledge base of computer terms and uses.	Whole class lesson followed by discussion on computer terms and uses of technology. List ways technology is used at home, at the workplace, and at school.	Use appropriate technology terminology; identify ways technology and computers have changed people's lives; identify and describe the characteristics of digital input, processing, and output.
Language Arts: Writing and composing; style—autobiography	Use multimedia encyclopedia, Internet, and word processor to copy and paste information for a class report. Print the report. Write an autobiography; use pictures from home to scan into the autobiography for illustrations.	Save and delete files; use menu options and commands; work with more than one software application (multi-tasking); name and describe the components which permit telecommunications including computers, modems, networks, phone lines, and servers; access remote equipment on a network, such as a printer or other peripheral.
Social Studies: Citizenship—follow directions; demonstrate care and respect in use of computer equipment	Use a variety of games and software to practice use of mouse and video display; practice use of devices to review tasks: record voice and play back, use word processor, demonstrate proper care of disk drives and disks.	Use a variety of input devices such as mouse, keyboard, disk drive, modem, voice/sound recorder, scanner, digital video, CD-ROM.
Computer Basics: Develop keyboarding proficiency in spelling, writing and composing, and word processing.	Use selected keyboarding software program for instruction; practice should support curriculum goals in language arts and other subjects; 6–8 weeks of intensive keyboarding lessons should be followed by a short review of skills at the beginning class all year long.	Use proper keyboarding techniques, such as correct hand/body position and smooth and rhythmic keystroke pattern; demonstrate touch keyboarding techniques for operating the alphabetic, numeric, symbol, and punctuation keys; show increasing speed on short timed tests.

Curriculum Area	Activity	Objective
Language Arts: Constructing meaning; writing and composing	Use computer for writing projects: fables, holiday stories, class reports and newsletters, friendly letters, thank you notes, invitations; proofread and edit work created in class; write stories and sentences with spelling words.	Produce documents at the keyboard: proofread and edit; apply language skills, including capitalization, punctuation, and symbol keys as grade-level appropriate; utilize the thesaurus.
Social Studies: Government/Citizenship; democratic decision making, respect for others and the environment	Design an Acceptable Use Policy for your school. Visit the Copyright Office at the Library of Congress: http://lcweb.loc.gov/copyright	Follow acceptable use policies; recognize that the Copyright law protects what a person, group, or company has created.
Computer Basics: Use, care and routine maintenance	Locate System Tools folder in the computer. Perform routine Scandisk and Disk Defrag throughout the year. Discuss the importance of virus protection.	Practice care in use of disks, computers, and supplies; recognize the need for protection of software and hardware from computer viruses; recognize that routine care and maintenance prevents computer problems.
Language Arts: Constructing meaning	Students use encyclopedia to research science and social studies topics from class curriculum.	Apply appropriate electronic search strategies to acquire information.
Health: Nutrition Computer tools: database	Search for information on nutrition and healthy eating on the Internet; create a database that will list foods by group; sort the database to create healthy menus with representatives from each group. Visit the "Clickable Pyramid" at www.nal.usda.gov:8001/py/pmap.htm to make choices.	Select appropriate strategies to navigate and access information on the Internet for research and resource sharing; create/modify an electronic database; search and sort information using one criterion; create a product using information located in a database.
Language Arts: Locating information	Make a scavenger hunt with encyclopedia. Students must find and write certain facts identified by the teacher.	Acquire information including text, audio, video, and graphics.

Curriculum Area	Activity	Objective
Social Studies: Government/citizenship	Locate the full-text version of The Declaration of Independence and the Constitution of the United States online. Discuss function and structure of U.S. Government as presented in the Constitution.	Determine usefulness and appropriateness of digital information.
Language arts: Locating information	Use multimedia encyclopedia to find information on space exploration; visit the NASA web site; use selected software to explore space.	Use software programs with audio, video, and graphics to enhance learning experiences.
Science: Space exploration **Math**: Graphing	Continue research about outer space through the Internet; visit the Nine Planets web site to view videos and animations; combine research to make a report about the preparations for a space shuttle mission; make a graph of the planets of our solar system and their moons.	Use appropriate software to express ideas and solve problems including use of word processing, graphics, databases, spreadsheets, simulations, and multimedia; use a variety of data types including text, graphics, digital audio, and video.
Health: Nutrition **Math**: Graphing	Discuss the importance of good nutrition; graph the foods served in the school cafeteria this week to determine if it meets the criteria for a healthy menu	Use communication tools to participate in group projects.
Social Studies: History **Science**: Ecosystems	Learn about Western Expansion and the California Gold Rush by playing "Oregon Trail"; visit the Oregon Trail web site; identify health, weather, and nutrition hardships faced by pioneers; identify the desert as an ecosystem, and list the problems it caused the pioneers in navigating through it.	Use interactive technology environments such as simulations, virtual museums field trips, or online interactive lessons to manipulate information.

Curriculum Area	Activity	Objective
Social Studies: Communities	Use e-mail as a way to reach out and connect to your national community from the school. Find schools in the web for student to communicate with from all parts of the country; visit the White House and e-mail the president; work as computer skills tutors with students in lower grades.	Participate with electronic communities as a learner, initiator, contributor, or mentor.
Language Arts: Style—Mythology and folklore	Search multimedia encyclopedia for articles on mythology and folklore; search Internet to read online selections of mythology, folklore, and fables; apply learning to write your own fable.	Apply appropriate electronic search strategies to acquire information.
Health: Diseases—communicable and non-communicable; bacteria and viruses	Search Internet for information on bacteria and viruses; identify health issues/diseases prevalent on the Oregon Trail; How could the pioneers have stayed healthier? What contributed to their diseases? Create a multimedia presentation as a class activity to present answers to these questions.	Design multimedia presentation that is appropriate for a defined audience and communicates the intent of subject matter.
Social Studies: Working together **Language Arts**: Writing and composing	Students work in groups to prepare a multimedia presentation on a selected state. Each group will prepare five slides to present to encourage others to visit that state.	Use presentation software to communicate with specific audiences.
Math: Charts and graphs	Identify the parts of a spreadsheet and discuss what it is used for; make a simple chart following written directions from teacher; view the results.	Use appropriate applications including spreadsheets and databases to develop charts and graphs by using data from various sources.

Curriculum Area	Activity	Objective
Language Arts: Writing and composing **Literature**: Style—newspaper article **Art**: Graphic design—creation and manipulation of computer-generated graphics	Create a class newsletter about the Oregon Trail as a group project. Pretend you are traveling the Oregon Trail. Write about things that may have taken place, and the things seen along the trail. Select and/or design graphics to illustrate articles.	Publish information in a variety of media including monitor display and printed copy.
Language Arts: Writing and composing - Students are given story starters to complete at selected times throughout the school year.	At the end of 1st, 3rd, and 5th grading periods, the student creates a project with the word processor and saves on floppy for teacher to evaluate. Student meets with teacher for conference on progress.	Select representative products to be collected and stored in an electronic evaluation tool; evaluate the product for relevance to the assignment or task.
Language Arts: Writing and composing **History**: Sequence of events **Literature**: Style—research report	Each child creates a timeline of the history of technology and the evolution of computers; search relevant topics in a multimedia encyclopedia; research and write report on the development of modern computers.	Create technology assessment tools to monitor progress of project such as checklists, timelines, or rubrics; explore the importance of telecommunications in today's world.

GLOSSARY OF TERMS FOR TEACHERS

acceptable use policy: A binding agreement signed by the user and, in the case of a K-12 student, also signed by the parent. The policy explains the rules of the Internet.

accessory programs: Programs Microsoft packages with Windows 95/98 including games (ex: Solitaire, Minesweeper), system tools (ex: disk defragmenter, scandisk) , and multimedia (ex: CD player, voice/sound recorder). They are available through the Start menu.

CD-ROM: Acronym for compact disk-read only memory, these disks may contain computer data and programs. They hold much more information than the once-traditional 3½ inch floppy disks for today's more graphic-intense applications. The CD-ROM player in your computer system will also play audio CD's.

clipboard: An area within the Windows interface that holds items that have been cut or copied from documents, including text, graphics, or sound.

CPU: The central processing unit of a computer system, it controls the system and processes all the information that goes through the machine.

copy: The process of sending a copy of an item such as a document or part of a document to the clipboard. From there you can send it somewhere else in the computer system.

cut: The process of removing an item such as a document or part of a document from somewhere in the computer system. The item that has been cut goes to the clipboard. From there you can send it somewhere else in the computer system.

database: A group of records that can be sorted according to certain descriptors or fields, including such items as address books, student lists, and attendance.

desktop: The Windows 95/98 background and screen.

desktop publishing program: A specialized software program which allows for the creation of a variety of documents from newsletters and brochures to worksheets and tickets. The process is completed through the creation of a series of frames for both text and graphics, so that the layout can be easily manipulated.

dialup networking: The configuration setting within your computer that allows the modem to dial a preset telephone number to connect with an Internet service provider.

disk defragmenter: A Windows 95/98 system tool that rearranges blank disk space left from deleted files or recently installed files. Defragmenting files allows your computer to access data more efficiently and more quickly.

disk drive: There are two kinds of disk drives in a computer. They include the hard disk drive which is non-removable, fast, and holds a great deal of information, and the floppy disk drive which is slower and does not hold as much information as a hard disk drive. The advantage of using a floppy disk is that it is removable and you can easily transfer and share data between two or more computers and perform backups of important information.

download: To copy a program or data from another computer to your own.

e-mail: Messages you can send electronically to others and are received by modem. E-mail stands for electronic mail.

E-Rate: Discounts allowed education facilities by the federal government for telecommunication connections. Its goal is to allow the teaching of technology literacy to all students.

font: A specific style of type. Some are fancy and others are plain.

format: The process of changing the appearance of a document. It may include changing the appearance of the font, applying borders, bullets, or changing the color of the text.

hardware: The physical devices of your computer that you can touch and see: system unit, disk and CD-ROM drives, keyboard, screen, printer, mouse.

hyperlink: Underlined and/or highlighted text within a web page that allows you to click on it to move to a site with related material.

icons: Small pictures that represent commands and programs in Windows 95/98.

input device: Any device within the computer system that allows for information to flow into the computer. Examples include: mouse, keyboard.

input/output device: Sometimes called I/O devices, these allow for the flow of information in both directions. Disk drives are I/O since data flows into the computer as you input it, and then you can retrieve the information to use again.

Internet Service Provider: Participation in this service is what allows you to make a connection to the Internet. As a customer of that provider, you are allowed to send and receive e-mail, browse the Web, and participate on the Internet.

LAN: Local Area Network-A group of computers that are locally connected on a network.

menu bar: The items (ex: file, edit, view) across the top of a Windows screen that allow you many choices for what you can do within any program.

modem: A device that allows your computer to connect to other computers over telephone lines. Using dialup networking with your modem will allow your computer to connect to your Internet service provider. Also, if you have the appropriate software installed on your computer, a modem will allow you to send and receive faxes.

multimedia: The capability of a computer to display graphics, motion video, and sound network: Any group of computers that can communicate and exchange information.

output device: Any device which allows information to flow out of the computer. These include the monitor display and printer.

Paint: The Windows 95/98 drawing program. It allows you to create a drawing that can then be inserted in another document.

paste: The process of sending the contents of the clipboard to another folder, document, or to the Windows desktop.

peripheral device: Any device attached externally to your computer which expand its capabilities. Examples of peripherals may include printers, scanners, speakers, monitors, pointing devices, and/or microphone. Peripherals are categorized as input or output devices.

plug-in: A "mini-program" that can be downloaded freely from the Internet which allows you to view multimedia on the Internet. Examples of plug-ins include: RealAudio, QuickTime, Flash, and Shockwave.

RAM: An acronym for Random Access Memory, it is the short-term memory in your computer. Typically, the more RAM you have, the faster your computer will run.

scan-converter: A device that allows for the connection of a television to a computer monitor for classroom display of computer activities.

ScanDisk: The Windows utility that allows for checking the disk drive for problems and potential problems, preventing future problems. The standard scan checks your disk for file errors. The thorough scan checks the files as well as doing a disk surface scan for any errors that may occur.

search engine: A web tool which allows you to search the Internet for specific information. Each engine has its own special features to allow you to present your question to find all kinds of information. Examples of search engines are AltaVista, Infoseek, Yahoo!, Excite, HotBot, Lycos, and WebCrawler.

software: A term used to describe the programs which may be installed on the hard drive of a computer.

scanner: A device that makes copies of photographs and documents. These copies may be saved to the hard drive for editing. Using photo enhancement software and special paper allows for the reproduction of photographs. Using OCR (optical character recognition) software allows for editing of scanned documents from within your computer.

spreadsheet: A document which allows for a number of different types of arithmetical calculations. An example would be a gradebook for calculating averages and grades.

Start Button: Located on the Windows 95/98 taskbar, this provides access to all the programs within a computer. The Start Menu takes the place of Windows 3.1x Program Manager.

taskbar: The bar on the Windows 95/98 desktop where running program icons appear. The system clock and Start button are located here also. Clicking on the program icon will activate that application.

Tool Bar: The icons under the menu bar that allow for performing certain actions without accessing the menu. Using these icons makes performing common tasks easier.

U.S.B.: Acronym for Universal Serial Bus, this is the newest technology for connecting peripheral devices to your computer system. It allows for easy installation of compatible hardware, and provides a much faster access from the computer to the peripheral. In addition, you can "daisy-chain" many devices to one plug through the use of a hub.

WAN: Wide Area Network—The network would cover a wide area, such as a county or a state.

web browser: Once connected to the Internet by an Internet Service Provider, this application allows for you to navigate and explore the Internet. Netscape Navigator and Internet Explorer are the two most commonly used web browsers.

Word Pad: Windows 95/98 basic word processor.

world wide web: The graphic interface that allows access to the Internet in a point-and-click manner, eliminating the need for extensive typed commands.

word processor: A program for creating professional looking documents by applying any number of formatting procedures to enhance the appearance of a document.

word wrap: The action of your cursor automatically moving to a new line when the previous line is full. This takes the place of the carriage return, used previously in typewriters.

SOFTWARE APPENDIX

Broderbund Company
"Where in the World is Carmen SanDiego?"
"Where in the U.S.A. is Carmen SanDiego?"

The Dole Company
"Five A Day" CD-ROM and
learning materials

Dorling Kindersley (DK Multimedia)
Eyewitness Encyclopedia of Space and the Universe
Dinosaur Hunter
My First Incredible, Amazing Dictionary

Encyclopedia Britannica
Britannica CD 99 Multimedia Edition

Grolier Interactive, Inc.
1999 Grolier Multimedia Encyclopedia

The Learning Company
Compton's Encyclopedia 99 Deluxe

MECC
Amazon Trail
Oregon Trail

Microsoft Corporation
Encarta Encyclopedia Deluxe 99
Magic School Bus Series
Works 4.5

Random House New Media
"Living Books" Series—Interactive stories on CD-ROM of library favorites

World Book
1999 World Book
Multimedia Encyclopedia

BIBLIOGRAPHY

"Challenges and Strategies in Using Technology to Promote Education Reform." U.S. Department of Education: Office of Educational Research and Improvement. Project Director—Dr. Ram Singh.
Available online at:
<http://www.ed.gov/pubs/EdReformStudies/EdTech/approaches.html>

Clinton, William Jefferson. "The President's Educational Technology Initiative." Excerpted from State of the Union Address to Congress. January 23, 1996.
Available online at:
<http://www.whitehouse.gov/WH/EOP/edtech/html/edtech_f.html>

Eisenberg, Michael B. and Doug Johnson. "Computer Skills for Information Problem-Solving: Learning and Teaching Technology in Context." Clearinghouse on Information and Technology. ERIC Digest EDO-IR-96-04. March, 1996.
Available online at:
<http://ericir.syr.edu/ithome/digest/computerskills.html>